Beautiful People

Emma Djukic

BookLeaf Publishing

India | USA | UK

Presentation by *BookLeaf Publishing*

Web: www.bookleafpub.com

E-mail: info@bookleafpub.com

ISBN: 978-93-5744-962-5

First edition 2022

DEDICATION

To those who feel like they are alone.

I am here.

I see you.

Do you see me too?

ACKNOWLEDGEMENT

I would like to begin by thanking my parents for never telling me to stop reading or writing. You were my first supporters, hvala vam za sve, dragi moji roditelji, mnogo vas volim. I also want to express my sincerest gratitude for the best editor I could ask for, Shailah Aggarson. You continue to choose me, to read my poems and make them better, and for that I love you. Thank you. And finally, I would like to thank BookLeaf Publishing for bringing my writing to life.

PREFACE

We write the stories we need to hear. The tale I needed to be true was one where I didn't lose in the end. And so, these poems, born from the well of emotions within me, are my gift to all those who feel as though they are lost, and there is no way out. May you enjoy reading them as I did writing them.

Soul Weary

I have gone numb
My kindness spent on those who don't return it
My energy torn apart by my demons
Time dissipates into thin air and I am in debt
Left with nothing but emptiness inside

And yet I nurse this void
For it is better to feel the lack of something
Than nothing at all
And I want to cry, but the tears won't come
For that takes more will than I have to give

If I call, will someone hear?
If they hear, will someone care?
This fear seals my lips
And I sit alone in the dark
With my pain barely holding me together

No one wants a broken person
And I am not worth the pity
Soul weary and tired,
My smiles grow harder to force
And I wish someone would notice
How paper-thin they truly are

Victim

How can you always think
It's an offence against you
My mere existence

It's not about you
I don't have the patience
To plan every slight
Nor time
To concoct every insult
I am too tired to take care of myself
Let alone scheme to make you miserable

And yet here we are again
Your blame finds me like an arrow
Piercing through my heart
And teaching me to turn it to stone

Don't you dare pretend
As though I don't love
That I am cold and broken
You made me this way
I hide from your words
The only way I know how

Giving

I become what you need
Its what I have always done
Been there for my friends
You say that you've never met someone like me
And neither have I
For who else gives you
Every part of themselves
Without ever demanding something in return

And when I finally draw a line
You recoil in disgust
Shaming me for wanting
A friendship
Some credit
For all that I am

And I am still not enough

Tired

At this point

It takes more effort

To tell you to stop

To leave me alone

Than to just wait

For you to get bored of me

Outside In

I've been watching you for years
Telling myself that I don't want your life
That your world is cruel and full of deceit
~You're better than that~ I whisper

And yet
And yet
And yet

Wouldn't it be wonderful to walk tall
Knowing that others wanted to be me?

Wouldn't it be grand to be desired?
For once?

Your laughter seems so much truer than mine
Even if I know that it is at someone else's
expense

Why can't I be stronger and move on
My eyes always flit back to you
From the outside of your world
Forever only looking in

Logos

We tried
You cannot say between two people like us
There wasn't patience and discipline

But my friend
I cannot treat love like I treat a logical argument

Deconstruct it
Put it in a box
And demand that it follows
      Rules
           Restrictions
                Regulations

Perhaps the timing created a divide
Between us

But I will not be settled for
We both deserve better
And maybe in another time you'll see
That a contract
Is not a relationship

What's in a Man?

His eyes no longer look my way
With wonder or with glee
Nor does his little hand seek mine
Instead it just hangs free

For he is not so little now
He's tall and proud and strong
Grown up into a fine young man
Who tries to do no wrong

But pride it is a wicked thing
That tells you that you're weak
When once you found my stories wild
You now won't let me speak

You wear your silence like a shield
And I can't make it through
I wish you'd let me in again
But this man is someone new

We all grow up and change with time
Grow into who we are
I miss the way we used to be
But you've travelled on so far

I cannot do this on my own
You were always on my side
Come back to me, my little boy
Don't let them make you hide

Storm

I cannot even tell you why I am angry
At all of it
None of it
Myself

I talk too much
In hopes of figuring out what is wrong
but I can't think in the midst of this tempest
And the growing chaos makes it harder to
breathe

I want to throw things
Punch them

I want to be held
And whispered to with love

I can't sit still
Looking out of windows
My foot taps in a discordant rhythm
Knowing it wants to lead me out
But there is nowhere to go
That will shelter me
From the storm within myself

Breaking Point

I closed my eyes
Put the pencil down
Pushed away from the desk
And left

Aftermath

I find myself in the fields again
Somehow, it always comes back to them
I lie in the grasses
Without a thought on my mind

And for the first time

In too long

I simply

Am

A Parent's Love

You never told me to speak softer
So I grew up with a voice full of confidence

You never told me to stop running
So I grew up knowing how to pace myself

You never told me I couldn't do it
And for that I am most grateful

I learned my own limits
You never forced them upon me

And so every success
I owe to the freedom I had
To grow into myself
All the while knowing
That you would be there to catch me
If I climbed too high

Words

As I child I would devour books
Settle between the pages in hopes of stealing to a
world
That seemed so much ~more~ than my own
And the glyphs which were my portal to these
places
Half-moons and lines
Words

Harmonious, ethereal, tragically beguiling
They leapt from the paper in my hand
To weave a fresco of life
I would sing these wonders of mine
These words that brought me so much joy
Out loud for all to hear
Not caring if they whispered

But as I grew up, my words felt out of place
Instead of laughter I found scorn
My stories of wilderness and romance
Did not appeal to those who claimed to have
grown up
And now found amusement in gossip
So I began to hold these treasures to my chest
Thinking it was what I had to do to be enough

It began with the little things
A phrase traded for an acronym
Kindness switched out for a tease
But then
I forgot how to spin a story from air
And a depth which had lived in me since I was a
child
Went dry
And my tears could not bring it back

You made me think that I had to choose
Between my words or your tolerance
I did not know then what I do now
And I believed that I had to give you this part of
me
That I was too much

But maybe
Just maybe
You are not enough

Buttons

We have come home now
From our honeymoon phase
It is over
And we learn to seek love in the mundane
Hand in hand with quiet smiles
Yet while walking through each other's lives
We find dusty places to stick our fingers
Into nooks where the buttons hide

I let you in, opening the door
A welcome to my life
But there are places I do not tread in this house
And you push me into the rooms
Not out of hate
Or malice
I know this
But my defences are trained
My reaction is sharp

Leave me alone
I cry
Don't press that one
I beg
How could someone I trusted betray me so

You find my buttons
More skillfully than I can hide them
But for the first time
They are not crushed
But loved

And you wipe the tears from my face
With the same kindness that earned you my trust
Oh how sweet you are to me
And all of my buttons

Mirrors

You are a better actor than I will ever be
Not because you love it
But because you love those around you
More than yourself

Or so you say

It is an excuse and you know it
It is easier to broil in misery
Than to pick yourself up and try again

And each time I comfort you I see in your eyes
A reflection
Of what I was
And of what I might become
If I let myself fall too far

But I pick myself up
And don't waste energy hiding my scars

I am not whole yet.

It took a while to learn
But my faults are not a weakness of my
character

They are a sign of my humanity

You close yourself off and become numb
But without feeling those emotions
You lose that part which makes you so much
more
Than broken

And so each time I walk past you now
I see less of a mirror
And more of a photograph of times past
I hope to help you see how I made it out
But I will not crumble into that void again with
you

Blank Page

I picked up a pen
For the first time in ages
Not to write for someone else
But for myself

And I didn't know where to start
There were so many things
So many half-thoughts
Racing through my mind

It was daunting
To begin again
When once it was so simple
Shame touched me for not being better

But I took a breath and started with one word
And then another
And another

Oh how silly I was to think
That time alone would cost you
A very part of your soul
I was wrong

Significance

It took me
~so long~
to realize that people don't care
Not about me
Not about you
Not about themselves, even

We are peculiar beings

For what we do doesn't matter
How you sit
How you laugh
What you find funny
Not really

And somehow that is okay
Because everyone else is too scared
Too anxious about their own problems
To even think about me

And it is liberating
To put value into my own being
Their recognition does not hold me up
But that makes it

All the more special
When you care to notice
The little ways that I am

Compromise

When do we start making compromises
And simply stop fighting for it all?
It is a blurred line that scares me

Because
I want to be chosen
I want to choose
I want to trust
That I mean enough to someone
To become
A ceaseless thought
A ravenous obsession that scorns all reason

I don't want to be your compromise
For you were never mine

Late Night Texts

How do you manage to make me feel
Like I matter in a world of billions
In this stolen night of ours

Adults

Tell me I'm insane
tell me I'm not allowed to be young
and in love with life
and to feel emotions in places
I didn't know could feel

In my throat
my eyes
My lips with every smile that is brought to them

I dare you
To tell me to be like you
Cold
stubborn
Aloof
You fear me
and you hide it behind your nonchalance

but oh how you quiver
At the thought of admitting
that you can't feel like I do anymore
I am young
And in love with life

Beautiful People

I sit a little taller now
My shoulders less burdened
With the weight of an invisible world

For when you choose your people
And they become the most important ones
Carrying only them in your heart
Is so simple
After the hell you have lived through

I see colours in the trees
As I walk on by
And I can't help but smile
Thinking with lightness

That there are good humans in this world
Kind souls
And they are rare, it is true

But life is so bleak
Without wonderful friends
To fill it with joys

And so I am thankful
For all the beautiful people
Who make me better

Epilogue

Looking at who I was
I cannot help but wish
That I could hug her
And tell her
That it will get better
Even though I know
She won't believe me

But she'll make it
So I walk on
Without looking back
Because there
Onward
Wait the versions of myself
I am yet to meet